Contents

Some words are shown in bold, **like this**.
You can find them in the glossary on page 23.

What is an octopus?

An octopus is an animal that lives in the ocean.

Octopuses live in oceans all over the world.

Pacific giant octopus

There are different types of octopus.

Some octopuses are tiny and some are very big.

What do octopuses look like?

mantle

An octopus has a soft body called a **mantle** and eight long arms.

If an octopus's arm is damaged, another one grows in its place.

sucker

The bottom of each octopus arm is covered with **suckers**.

An octopus uses its suckers to grip things tightly and to touch and taste.

What do octopuses do at night?

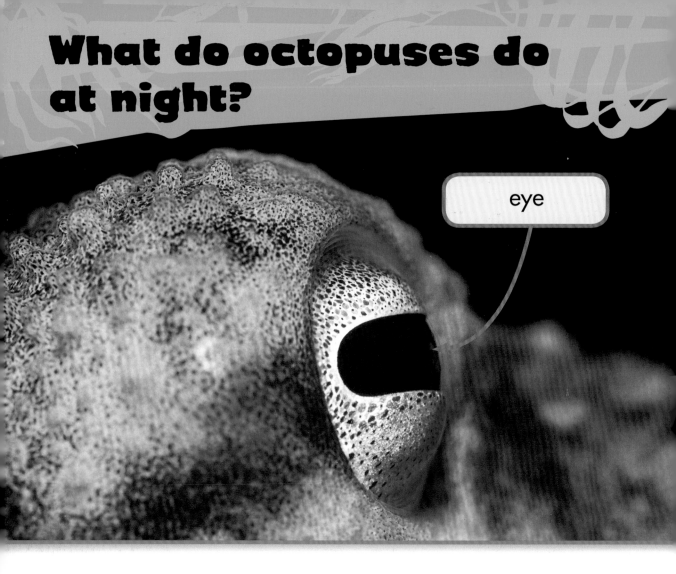

eye

Most octopuses hunt for food at night.

Octopuses can see very well, even in the dark.

Octopuses look for places where food might be at night.

They use their arms to explore using touch and taste.

How does an octopus move?

An octopus can walk along the sea floor on its arms.

It pulls itself along with the rows of **suckers** on the underside of its arms.

To swim, an octopus sucks water into its body.

Then it shoots the water out again to move quickly through the sea.

What does an octopus eat?

crab

Octopuses eat crabs, sea snails, fish, turtles, and even other octopuses.

The giant octopus may eat small sharks.

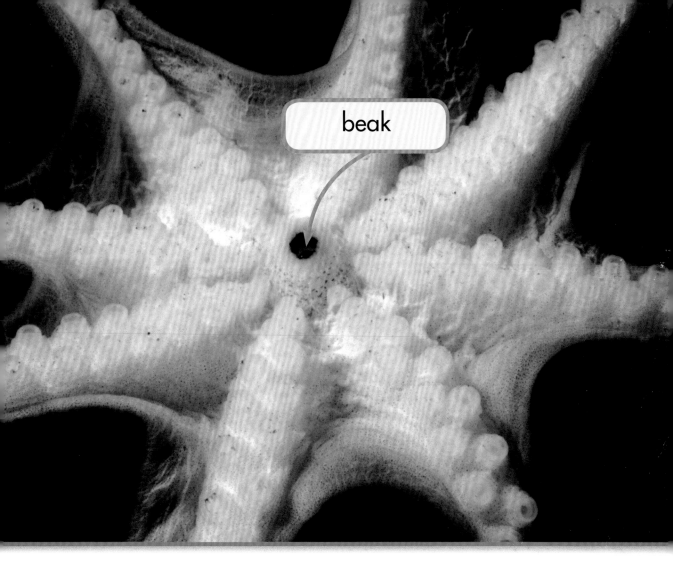

beak

An octopus has a hard sharp **beak** inside its mouth.

This beak can bite into thick shells and break food into small pieces.

How do octopuses hunt?

An octopus can squeeze its arms inside holes or cracks in rock.

Its **suckers** feel around for food and grab it.

crab

When an octopus uses its **beak** to bite an animal, it also puts **venom** into it.

Venom is a poison that kills the animal so the octopus can eat it.

What do octopuses do all day?

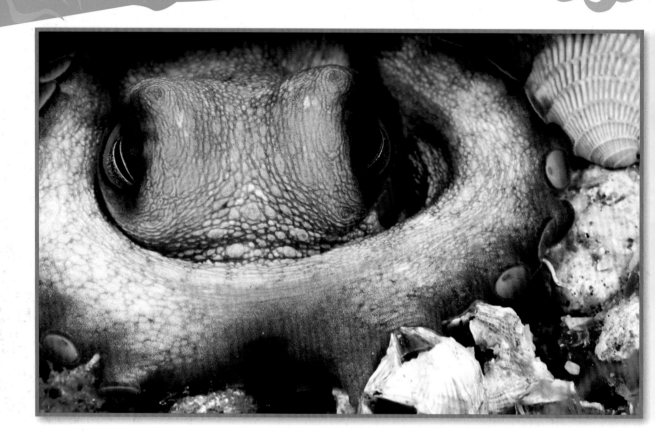

Most octopuses rest alone in their **dens** during the day.

Octopus dens are spaces in rocks or holes in the sea floor.

Outside their dens, many octopuses can change colour to look like rock or sand.

This **camouflage** keeps them hidden from animals that might try to eat them.

What are octopus babies like?

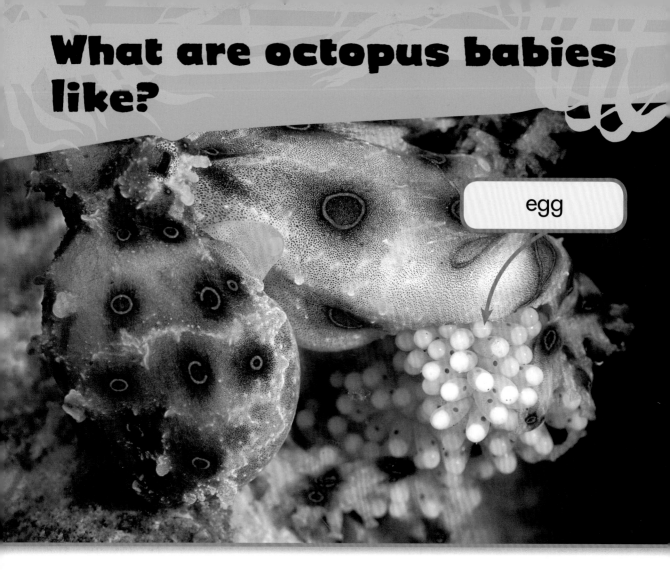

egg

A mother octopus lays **eggs** in her **den**.

She looks after the eggs for months and never leaves the den to feed.

baby octopus

Tiny baby octopuses hatch from the eggs.

They leave the den to live alone and their mother dies.

What hunts octopuses?

octopus

Sea lions, some dolphins, large eels, and sharks hunt octopuses.

Octopuses often use **camouflage** to hide from these animals outside their **dens**.

ink

When an animal attacks an octopus, the octopus squirts black ink from its body.

This black cloud hides the octopus and it can swim away quickly.

Octopus body map

mantle

eyes

arms

suckers

Glossary

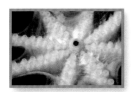 **beak** mouth that is made up of two hard, pointed parts that close together

 **camouflage** when an animal's body colour blends in with its surroundings

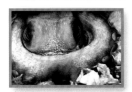 **den** crack or hole in rock or sea floor where an octopus rests and lays its eggs

 **egg** small, rounded object that contains a baby animal

 **mantle** main part of an octopus body, which looks like a bag

 **sucker** cup-shaped part on an octopus's arm that sucks and grips onto things

 **venom** poisonous juice that can kill animals

Find out more

Books

Octopuses (Under the Sea), Carol K. Lindeen (Capstone Press, 2005)

Octopuses and Squids (Undersea Encounters), Mary Jo Rhodes and David Hall (Children's Press, 2006)

Websites

Meet lots of different types of octopus at: **video.kids.nationalgeographic. com/video/player/kids/animals-pets-kids/wild-detectives-kids/wd-ep1-octopus.html**

Watch a video on the North Pacific giant octopus at: **www.bbc.co.uk/ nature/species/North_Pacific_Giant_Octopus**

Index